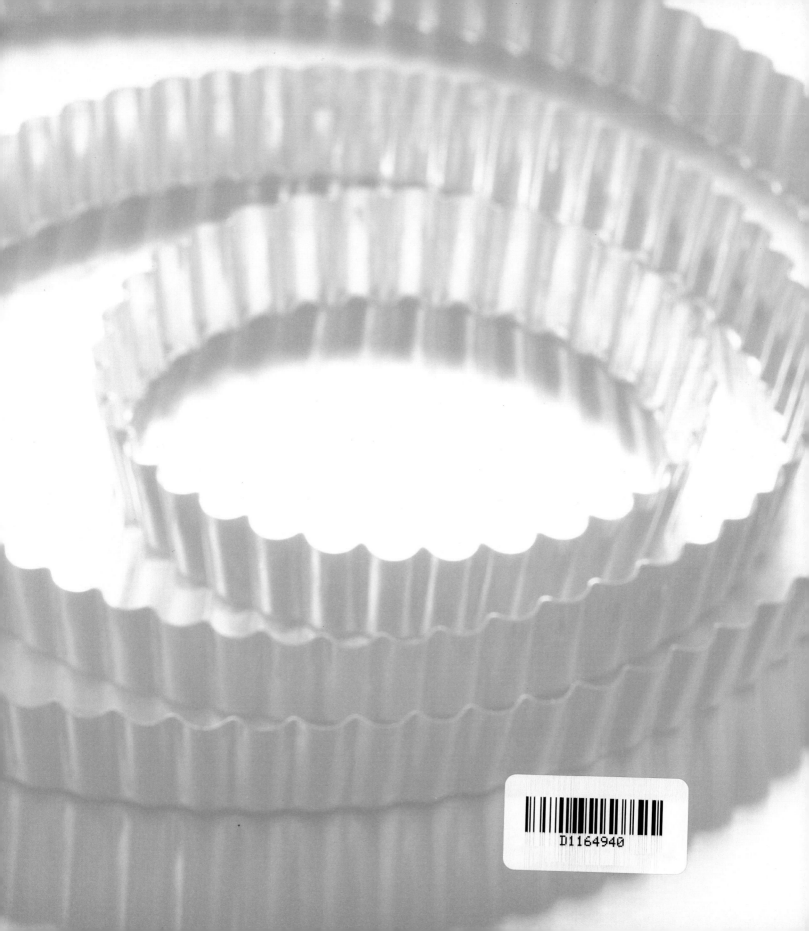

cakes, cookies,
pies & tarts

WILLIAMS-SONOMA

cakes, cookies, pies & tarts

WELDON OWEN

contents

1

2

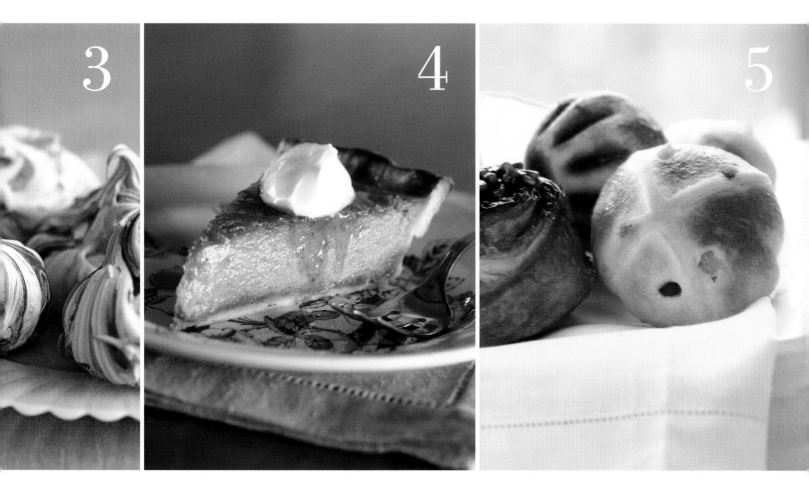

introduction

A journey into the land of milk and honey (and nuts and chocolate), a sweet adventure with irresistible results, awaits within these pages. This collection of dessert recipes gathers innovative and exciting creations from around the globe, along with interesting takes on familiar favorites. Chosen for their exquisite taste, they also delight the eyes. Consider this book an ode to pleasure with instructions on how to prepare and enjoy lovely desserts.

—chuck williams

fruit desserts

Some might argue that a choice piece of fruit needs no adornment—and sometimes they are right. But for those occasions when a ripe fig or crisp apple is not enough, a fruit fool or sorbet, a little roasted or poached fruit in wine can provide just the answer. From spring rhubarb to late-fall pears, fruits mirror the passing seasons, offer a rainbow of possibilities, and provide a luscious and refreshing end to any meal.

Plum and Goat Cheese Terrine with Gingersnap Crust

A simple seasonal dessert, this can be made with almost any fruit, from nectarines and peaches to strawberries, figs, or even dried apricots.

12 gingersnaps (2½ oz/75 g)

3½ tablespoons unsalted butter, melted

3½ tablespoons sugar

3 or 4 plums

½ lb (250 g) soft, spreadable mild fresh goat cheese, at room temperature

2 tablespoons heavy (double) cream, plus more if needed

3 tablespoons apricot jam, melted and sieved

SERVES 4

1 In a blender or food processor, process gingersnaps to fine crumbs. Transfer to a bowl. Add melted butter and 1 tablespoon sugar and mix. Transfer to a 6-inch (15-cm) springform pan and press down with your fingers to make a solid layer. Transfer to freezer and chill until firm, about 15 minutes.

2 Slice plums very thinly and discard pits. Reserve enough of best slices to form an overlapping spiral pattern on top of terrine. In a small saucepan, combine remaining plum slices, remaining 2½ tablespoons sugar, and 2½ tablespoons water. Bring to a boil over medium-high heat and cook, crushing fruit with a fork, until thickened to a chunky sauce, about 5 minutes. Remove from heat and let cool.

3 In a bowl, combine goat cheese and cream, mashing together to produce a spreadable consistency. Mixture should be creamy but should hold its shape; if it is too stiff, add a little more cream. Cover cookie crust in pan with ½ cup (4 oz/125 g) goat cheese mixture, spreading it to form a ½-inch (12-mm) layer. Spread plum sauce over cheese layer. Top with a layer of remaining goat cheese mixture and smooth surface. Top with an overlapping spiral design of sliced plums. Brush fruit with melted apricot jam.

4 Cover with plastic wrap and refrigerate for at least 1 hour or until ready to serve. Remove plastic and run a knife around edges of terrine, then remove pan sides.

Rhubarb Sorbet

1 cup (8 oz/250 g) sugar

1 lb (500 g) rhubarb, thinly sliced, about 3½ cups

SERVES 6–8

This sorbet tastes best when made with the amount of sugar given here, but it must be eaten shortly after it comes out of the ice-cream maker. If it is to be kept overnight, increase the sugar to 1½ cups (12 oz/375 g), to keep the sorbet from freezing too hard.

1 In a saucepan, combine sugar and 1½ cups (12 fl oz/375 ml) water. Bring to a boil over medium heat, stirring occasionally, until sugar is dissolved. Remove from heat and set aside.

2 Meanwhile, in another saucepan, combine rhubarb and ¼ cup (2 fl oz/60 ml) water. Cover and cook over very low heat, stirring occasionally, until rhubarb falls apart, about 15 minutes. Do not allow to burn.

3 In a food processor, purée rhubarb.

4 Stir rhubarb purée into sugar syrup. Refrigerate for at least 5 hours.

5 Freeze in an ice-cream maker according to manufacturer's instructions.

Compote of Peaches with Ginger and Star Anise

Spooned into goblets or served on dessert plates with crisp cookies and crème fraîche, compote is a subtle finish to a meal.

12 peaches,
about 4 lb (2 kg) total weight

2 cups (16 fl oz/500 ml)
Chenin Blanc

½ cup (4 oz/250 g) sugar

1 vanilla bean, halved lengthwise

1-inch (2.5-cm) piece ginger,
peeled and thinly sliced

3 star anise pods

SERVES 8

1 Bring a large saucepan three-fourths full of water to a boil and fill a large bowl with ice and water. Immerse peaches in boiling water for 30 seconds. Using a slotted spoon, transfer to bowl of ice water to cool, then peel off skin.

2 Using a small, sharp knife, cut each peach in half down to the pit, cutting through stem end and following slight ridge along side of peach. Grasp halves of cut peach and twist gently, pulling them apart. Remove and discard pit. If pit clings to peach, use knife to carefully pry or cut it out.

3 In a saucepan large enough to hold the peaches, combine 1 cup (8 fl oz/250 ml) water, wine, sugar, vanilla bean, ginger, and star anise. Bring to a boil over medium heat, stirring to dissolve sugar. Boil until a light syrup forms, 4–5 minutes.

4 Reduce heat to a simmer. Gently slip peaches into syrup and poach for about 5 minutes. Using a slotted spoon, transfer peaches to a bowl. Pour syrup over fruit and let stand for several hours, turning occasionally. Serve at room temperature, chilled, or reheated.

Figs Stuffed with Gorgonzola

2 tablespoons caraway seeds

12 ripe figs

1½ tablespoons extra-virgin olive oil

¼ cup (1 oz/30 g) Gorgonzola

¼–⅓ cup (3–4 oz/90–125 g)
lavender honey

SERVES 4

Figs stuffed with rich, creamy Gorgonzola and roasted to bursting sweetness make an unusual fall dessert. The combination of the slightly resinous taste of honey and the earthy flavor of caraway is wonderful. Choose figs that are soft to the touch, which have the fully developed sugars lacking in firm figs.

1 Preheat oven to 400°F (200°C).

2 In a frying pan, toast caraway seeds over medium heat, shaking pan, until fragrant, about 3 minutes. Be careful not to burn them. Set aside.

3 Rub figs all over with olive oil, then make a lengthwise slit in each fig and insert about 1 teaspoon cheese in each. Place stuffed figs, slit end up, on a baking sheet.

4 Bake until figs are plump and shiny but have not burst, about 10 minutes.

5 Meanwhile, drizzle a little honey on each dessert plate and place about 1½ teaspoons caraway seeds alongside, leaving room for figs. To serve, place 3 figs on each plate.

Blackberry Fool
with Fruit Salad

2 cups (8 oz/250 g) fresh
blackberries

1½ cups (12 fl oz/375 ml) heavy
(double) cream

½ cup (4 oz/125 g) crème fraîche

¼ cup (1 oz/30 g) confectioners'
(icing) sugar

1 teaspoon rose water

1 small melon, such as pepino,
peeled, quartered, and seeded

2 firm but ripe peaches,
halved and pitted

2 firm but ripe nectarines,
halved and pitted

SERVES 6

Fools are a classic British dessert, made by folding cooked puréed fruit into a generous amount of whipped cream. Crushed fresh blackberries refresh this dessert, enhanced by the addition of a fruit salad alongside.

1 Set aside 18 blackberries. Put remaining blackberries in a bowl and, with back of a wooden spoon, gently crush.

2 In a large bowl, combine cream, crème fraîche, confectioners' sugar, and rose water. Using an electric mixer, beat until stiff peaks form; do not overbeat. Fold in crushed blackberries. Cover and refrigerate until ready to serve.

3 Using a mandoline or sharp knife, slice melon, peaches, and nectarines ⅛ inch (3 mm) thick. Divide fruit among dessert plates. Spoon a generous dollop of blackberry fool on top of fruit and garnish with reserved blackberries.

Mixed Berry Crumble

For this simple crumble, use either a single type of berry or a combination of favorites. It is equally delicious accompanied by lightly sweetened whipped cream, a dollop of crème fraîche, or a scoop of vanilla ice cream.

3 cups (12 oz/375 g)
mixed fresh berries

2 tablespoons balsamic vinegar

10 tablespoons (5 oz/150 g) sugar

1½ cups (7½ oz/235 g)
all-purpose (plain) flour

½ cup (4 oz/125 g) cold unsalted
butter, cut into small pieces

pinch of salt

SERVES 4

1 Preheat oven to 400°F (200°C). In a bowl, toss berries with balsamic vinegar and 4 tablespoons (2 oz/60 g) sugar. Let stand for 30 minutes.

2 In a food processor, pulse together remaining 6 tablespoons (3 oz/90 g) sugar, flour, butter, and salt until mixture resembles fine bread crumbs. Do not over-work mixture or it will turn into pastry.

3 Divide berry mixture among four 1-cup (8–fl oz/250-ml) ovenproof dishes or ramekins. Sprinkle crumble mixture over berries. Shake dishes slightly to allow ingredients to settle. Bake until top is golden, about 30 minutes.

Tomato Confiture

1½ lb (750 g) ripe tomatoes, cored and bottoms scored with an X

2½ cups (20 oz/625 g) sugar

¼ vanilla bean, split

MAKES 2 CUPS (16 FL OZ/500 ML)

Serve as a simple dessert, with fromage blanc or a fresh goat's or sheep's milk cheese, or use as a topping on poached pears, or with muffins, biscuits, or toast. Keep in the refrigerator, in a sealed container, for up to a week.

1 In a large pot of boiling water, blanch tomatoes in batches until skins loosen, about 15 seconds. Drain and rinse with cold water. Slip off skins and cut each tomato in half crosswise. Gently squeeze out seeds, then cut tomatoes into small pieces. Set aside.

2 In a nonreactive, heavy saucepan, combine sugar and 1 cup (8 fl oz/250 ml) water. Bring to a boil over high heat, stirring carefully, until sugar is dissolved. Add tomatoes, reduce heat to a simmer, and cook, stirring frequently, for 30 minutes.

3 Add vanilla bean and continue simmering until thickened and beginning to jell, 25–30 minutes. Test with a candy thermometer, which should register 220–222°F (104–106°C), or spoon a little jam on a chilled plate, let stand for a few minutes, and slide a finger through; if surface wrinkles, the jam has jelled.

4 Skim any foam from top, discard vanilla bean, and let cool completely before serving.

Baked Peaches with Pistachios

4 firm but ripe freestone peaches,
rinsed well and patted dry

2 egg yolks

1 tablespoon sugar

¾ teaspoon unsweetened
cocoa powder

⅛ teaspoon vanilla extract
(essence)

8 amaretti cookies,
coarsely crumbled

2 tablespoons shelled
pistachios, chopped

½ cup (4 fl oz/125 ml) Muscat
or other sweet wine

SERVES 4

The crunchy cookie filling resembles the pit of a peach. Top each serving with a dollop of whipped cream, crème fraîche, or mascarpone, and garnish with a fresh mint sprig.

1 Preheat oven to 400°F (200°C).

2 Using a small, sharp knife, cut each peach in half down to the pit, cutting through stem end and following slight ridge along side of peach. Grasp halves of cut peach and twist gently, pulling them apart. Remove and discard pit. With a melon baller, remove a little flesh from center of each peach half, forming a larger cavity. Chop peach trimmings finely.

3 In a bowl, combine egg yolks, sugar, cocoa powder, and vanilla. Whisk until smooth. Stir in chopped peach, cookie crumbs, and pistachios.

4 Pour Muscat into a buttered shallow 2-qt (2-l) baking dish. Arrange peaches halves, cut side up, in baking dish. Stuff each peach cavity with cookie mixture, mounding slightly. Bake, basting once or twice with cooking juices, until peaches are soft but still hold their shape and filling is firm and lightly browned, 20–25 minutes.

5 Place 2 peach halves on each dessert plate and drizzle with cooking juices. Serve warm.

Quinces Poached in Wine Syrup

Poached quinces in syrup can be stored in the refrigerator for weeks. Serve with freshly churned vanilla ice cream or Italian panna cotta.

2 cups (16 fl oz/500 ml) Muscat wine, such as Essencia Orange Muscat

2 cups (1 lb/500 g) sugar

1 cinnamon stick

3 whole cloves

¼ teaspoon peppercorns

5 golden quinces, about 2 lb (1 kg), peeled, cored, and cut into slices ¾ inch (2 cm) thick

SERVES 10

1 In a saucepan, combine wine, sugar, spices, and 4 cups (32 fl oz/1 l) water. Bring to a boil over medium heat, stirring to dissolve sugar. Add quinces and return to a boil.

2 Reduce heat to medium-low and place parchment (baking) paper on surface to cover. Simmer gently until quinces are tender and pink, about 2½ hours. If syrup seems thin, remove fruit with a slotted spoon and reduce syrup to desired consistency. Serve very cold.

Rose Quince Spread

Quince spread can be served with rustic country breads or biscuits for breakfast, with scones for a sweet treat, or accompanied with mature cheddar cheese. It will keep in the refrigerator, in a sealed container, for a week or so.

1 lb (500 g) golden quinces, fuzz rubbed off and rinsed

2 cups (1 lb/500 g) sugar

finely grated zest of 1 orange

2 rose geranium leaves or a dash of rose water

1–2 teaspoons apple cider vinegar, to taste

MAKES 2½ CUPS (20 FL OZ/625 ML)

1 In a food processor or by hand, coarsely grate quinces, or cut by hand into narrow julienne. Wrap cores and seeds in cheesecloth (muslin) and tie like a bouquet garni.

2 In a saucepan, combine sugar and 4 cups (32 fl oz/1 l) water. Bring to a boil over medium-high heat, stirring to dissolve sugar. Add quinces. When syrup returns to a boil, push quince shreds into syrup until they become saturated enough to stay below surface. Add cheesecloth bundle, orange zest, and rose geranium leaves. If using rose water, do not add at this time.

3 Reduce heat to medium-low and simmer until quinces turn rosy pink, about 1½ hours. Remove cheesecloth bundle and let quince mixture stand overnight.

4 The next day, taste quince mixture and add vinegar to sharpen flavor if desired. Bring to a boil, reduce heat to low, and cook until consistency of runny honey, 45–60 minutes. Remove rose geranium leaves or stir in rose water if using.

5 Let cool completely before serving.

Grape and Plum Cobbler

2½ cups (15 oz/470 g) mixed green and red seedless grapes

2 plums, halved, pitted and thinly sliced

2 teaspoons fresh lemon juice

6 tablespoons (3 oz/90 g) sugar

2 tablespoons all-purpose (plain) flour

CRUST

1 cup (5 oz/155 g) all-purpose (plain) flour

2 tablespoons sugar

1¼ teaspoons baking powder

¼ teaspoon salt

¼ cup (2 oz/60 g) cold unsalted butter, cut into small pieces

¼ cup (2 fl oz/60 ml) milk

SERVES 6

Grapes are delicious cooked, and they make a very good cobbler. Different colors and varieties can be mixed, or the cobbler can be made from a single variety. The same is true of the plums, which add extra flavor and texture. Serve this warm with a big scoop of vanilla ice cream–and, if any cobbler is left over, eat it for breakfast the next day.

1 In a bowl, combine grapes, plums, and lemon juice. In a small bowl, stir sugar and flour together, then sprinkle over fruit, tossing to coat. Set aside.

2 FOR CRUST: Preheat oven to 450°F (230°C). In a bowl, stir flour, sugar, baking powder, and salt together. Add butter and, using a pastry blender or 2 knives, cut butter into flour mixture until pea-sized pieces form. Using a fork, gradually stir in milk, mixing just until dough sticks together. Gather dough into a ball. On a floured work surface, pat dough into an 8-inch (20-cm) square.

3 Gently transfer fruit and its juices to an 8-inch (20-cm) square baking dish. Lay dough over top. Place dish on a rimmed baking sheet.

4 Bake for 20 minutes. Reduce oven temperature to 300°F (150°C) and continue to bake until juices are bubbling in dish, fruit is soft, and crust is well browned, about 15 minutes.

5 Remove from oven and let cool slightly. Serve warm or at room temperature, scooped from dish.

Rose and Strawberry Jelly

This easy and fresh fruit dessert is more gelatin than jam. The rose water gives this recipe a grown-up feel.

5 cups (1¼ lb/625 g) fresh strawberries, hulled and thinly sliced

½ cup (4 oz/125 g) sugar

1 envelope plain gelatin

1 teaspoon rose water

SERVES 4

1 In a bowl, combine 4 cups (1 lb/500 g) berries and sugar. Let stand for 2 hours. Strain through a medium-mesh sieve, pressing on berries with back of a large spoon to extract liquid. Discard solids. There will be about 1 cup (8 fl oz/250 ml) juice.

2 In another bowl, sprinkle gelatin over ¼ cup (2 fl oz/60 ml) water. Let stand until softened, 5 minutes. Add ¾ cup (6 fl oz/180 ml) boiling water and stir to dissolve gelatin. Add strawberry juice and rose water. Refrigerate until starting to set, about 1½ hours.

3 Divide remaining strawberries among individual serving glasses. Divide jelly evenly among glasses. Refrigerate until set, approximately 2 hours.

German Apple Pancake

This pancake is heavenly after a day of skiing or other cold-weather fun. Do not open the oven during the first 10 minutes of baking, or the pancake might fall. This pancake can also be served for breakfast.

PANCAKE

½ cup (2½ oz/75 g) all-purpose (plain) flour

½ teaspoon salt

3 eggs, at room temperature

½ cup (4 fl oz/125 ml) whole milk

2 tablespoons unsalted butter

½ tart apple, such as Granny Smith, peeled, cored, and thinly sliced

1 tablespoon firmly packed dark brown sugar

pinch of freshly grated nutmeg

TOPPING

¼ cup (2 oz/60 g) unsalted butter, melted

¼ cup (2 fl oz/60 ml) fresh lemon juice

confectioners' (icing) sugar

MAKES 1 LARGE PANCAKE; SERVES 2

1 FOR PANCAKE: Preheat oven to 475°F (245°C). Sift flour and salt together into a bowl.

2 In another bowl, whisk eggs and milk together until frothy and light. Gradually whisk egg mixture into flour mixture, just to blend. Do not overbeat.

3 In a 10-inch (25-cm) cast-iron skillet, melt butter over medium heat. Add apple and brown sugar. Sauté until apple is tender, 3–5 minutes. Sprinkle with nutmeg.

4 Pour batter over apple and place pan in oven. Bake until puffed and browned on edges, about 15 minutes, checking after 10 minutes.

5 Remove from oven. Place a serving platter over skillet. Carefully and quickly invert pancake onto platter, or serve directly from skillet.

6 FOR TOPPING: Drizzle pancake with melted butter and lemon juice. Dust with confectioners' sugar. Serve at once.

custards & puddings

Eggs, milk, and sugar are essential ingredients in the sweet kitchen, and from this heavenly trio come many riches. Combined and cooked on top of the stove or in the oven, they become custard or crème caramel; fold in whipped cream and you have mousse; add flour and the possibilities increase: soufflé, crêpe, or steamed pudding. However you combine them, a certain alchemy takes place and one spoonful is sure to lead to another.

Chocolate Soufflé

An elegant finale to any menu, this delectable soufflé is quite simple to prepare. Be sure to use good-quality chocolate.

¾ cup (6 fl oz/180 ml) plus 2 tablespoons whole milk

3 tablespoons plus ½ cup (4 oz/125 g) granulated sugar, plus more for coating ramekins

1½ tablespoons cornstarch (cornflour)

3 egg yolks

2½ oz (75 g) unsweetened baking chocolate, chopped

3½ tablespoons all-purpose (plain) flour

melted unsalted butter, for coating ramekins

6 egg whites

confectioners' (icing) sugar, for dusting

SERVES 6

1 In a small saucepan over medium heat, warm ¾ cup milk. While milk is heating, in a small bowl, combine remaining 2 tablespoons milk, 3 tablespoons granulated sugar, cornstarch, and egg yolks and whisk until blended.

2 When milk is about to boil, stir 2 tablespoons of the hot milk into egg mixture, then add all of egg mixture to milk and whisk thoroughly. Add chocolate and cook, whisking constantly, until mixture thickens, 45–60 seconds. Remove from heat and pour into a large bowl. Press a piece of plastic wrap directly on surface to prevent a skin from forming. Let cool. When mixture has cooled completely, stir in flour until blended.

3 Preheat oven to 375°F (190°C). Lightly brush insides of six 1¼-cup (10–fl oz/310-ml) soufflé ramekins with melted butter, then coat with granulated sugar.

4 In a bowl, using an electric mixer, beat egg whites on high speed until whites start to thicken, about 2 minutes.

5 Gradually add remaining ½ cup granulated sugar and continue to beat until whites are stiff and glossy, 1–2 minutes longer.

6 Add one-fourth of beaten egg whites to chocolate mixture and, using a rubber spatula, fold them in. Add remaining egg whites and fold in just until blended; some white streaks are acceptable. Finished mixture should be a very light, foamy batter.

7 Fill each prepared ramekin three-fourths full with soufflé batter. Place ramekins on a baking sheet and bake until soufflés have risen 1–2 inches (2.5–5 cm) above the edges of ramekins and tops are firm to the touch, 15–20 minutes. If baked for 15 minutes, soufflés will be moist in centers; if baked for 20 minutes, result will be a more cakelike consistency.

8 Sift confectioners' sugar over tops. Serve immediately.

Orange Custard

1½ cups (12 oz/375 g) sugar

6 whole eggs or 8 egg yolks

grated zest of 2 oranges

1 cup (8 fl oz/250 ml) fresh
orange juice

orange segments, for garnish

SERVES 6

This very sweet Sephardic flan is ideal for a kosher meal because it uses orange juice instead of milk or cream and therefore can be served after meat-based dishes. Individual ramekins work well, but you can also use small ovenproof bowls.

1 In a small, heavy saucepan, combine ½ cup (4 oz/125 g) sugar and 2 table-spoons water over high heat. Swirl pan to melt sugar. Cook, without stirring, until caramel colored and fragrant. Do not let caramel get too dark, or it will taste bitter. Carefully pour into a 3-cup (24–fl oz/750-ml) flan mold or six ¾-cup (6–fl oz/180-ml) individual custard cups. Swirl quickly to coat bottom and sides.

2 Preheat oven to 350°F (180°C).

3 In a bowl, whisk eggs with remaining 1 cup (8 oz/250 g) sugar. Add zest and orange juice. Mix well.

4 Pour mixture into prepared mold or custard cups. Place in a baking pan. Pour hot water into pan to come halfway up side of mold or cups. Cover baking pan with aluminum foil.

5 Bake until a knife inserted into center of custard comes out clean, 35–40 minutes for cups and 1 hour for mold. Remove mold or cups from baking pan. Let custard cool slightly. Cover with foil or plastic wrap. Refrigerate until well chilled.

6 Run a thin knife blade around edge of each cup or mold. Invert onto individual plates or 1 large plate. Spoon caramel over top. Top with orange segments.

Steamed Bittersweet
Chocolate Pudding

¾ cup (4 oz/125 g) all-purpose
(plain) flour

¾ teaspoon baking powder

3 tablespoons cocoa powder

pinch of salt

¼ cup (2 oz/60 g) unsalted butter,
softened

6 tablespoons (3 oz/90 g)
firmly packed light brown sugar

1 egg

½ teaspoon vanilla extract (essence)

½ cup (4 fl oz/125 ml) milk,
at room temperature

1 tablespoon instant espresso
dissolved in 1 tablespoon hot water

4 oz (125 g) bittersweet chocolate,
melted, plus 1 oz (30 g) bittersweet
chocolate, melted and slightly cooled

¼ cup (2 oz/60 g) granulated sugar

⅔ cup (5 fl oz/160 ml) cold
heavy (double) cream

2 teaspoons confectioners'
(icing) sugar

2 tablespoons best-quality bourbon

SERVES 8

Steamed puddings are traditional desserts, although there is nothing old-fashioned about this one. Chocolate lovers will be delighted.

1 Generously butter a 1-qt (1-l) pudding mold. In a small bowl, sift together flour, baking powder, 2 tablespoons cocoa powder, and salt. Set aside.

2 In a bowl, cream butter and brown sugar. Add egg and vanilla and beat well. Alternately stir in flour mixture and milk, beginning and ending with flour mixture. Stir in espresso and 4 oz melted chocolate. Pour batter into prepared mold and cover with lid. If mold does not have a lid, cover with a round of parchment (baking) paper and then aluminum foil, and secure with a rubber band.

3 Place a folded kitchen towel in center of a large pot. Place mold on towel and pour in boiling water to halfway up side of mold. Cover pot and simmer over low heat for 1½ hours, or until pudding has set and a knife inserted into center comes out clean. Remove pudding mold from water bath and let cool for 15 minutes.

4 Meanwhile, combine granulated sugar, remaining 1 tablespoon cocoa powder, and ¼ cup (2 fl oz/60 ml) water in a small saucepan. Bring to a boil, whisk to dissolve cocoa powder, and simmer for 5 minutes. Set aside.

5 Invert slightly cooled pudding onto a wire rack placed over a baking pan. While pudding is still warm, brush surface generously with cocoa syrup. Carefully transfer to a serving plate.

6 In a bowl, whisk cream, confectioners' sugar, and bourbon until soft peaks form. Whisk half of whipped cream into 1 oz slightly cooled melted chocolate to lighten. Immediately whisk in remaining whipped cream. Serve at once with pudding.

Rice Pudding
with Honey Meringue

½ cup (3½ oz/105 g) basmati rice

½ cup (3½ oz/105 g) Arborio rice
or other short-grain rice

⅛ teaspoon salt

1 cinnamon stick, plus ground
cinnamon for garnish

5 whole cardamom pods

3 whole cloves

3 cups (24 fl oz/750 ml) milk

1 teaspoon finely grated
orange zest

2 eggs, separated

1 tablespoon sugar

¾ cup (9 oz/280 g) orange
blossom or wildflower honey

1 teaspoon orange flower
water, or more to taste

2 tablespoons pistachio nuts,
skinned, lightly toasted,
and coarsely chopped

SERVES 8-10

Two kinds of rice are used in this delicate pudding–basmati for its flavor and fragrance and Arborio for its starchy texture. In an unusual twist on tradition, the pudding is lightened with a simple meringue made of egg whites and heavenly-scented orange blossom honey.

1 In a large saucepan, combine rices with 2½ cups (20 fl oz/625 ml) water and bring to a boil. Add salt. Reduce heat to medium-low and simmer, stirring often, until most of liquid has evaporated, about 15 minutes.

2 Meanwhile, tie cinnamon stick, cardamom, and cloves in a small piece of damp cheesecloth (muslin) to form a spice bag. Add to rice along with milk and orange zest. Raise heat to high and bring to a simmer, then reduce to low and cook, stirring often, until rice is soft and milk is nearly absorbed, about 18 minutes. Discard spice bag.

3 In a small bowl, whisk egg yolks with sugar until lemon colored. Quickly stir egg mixture into rice. Cook for 1 minute longer, stirring constantly. Transfer pudding to a large bowl and let cool.

4 Beat egg whites until stiff. Add honey and continue beating until glossy and thick. Fold into rice along with orange flower water and most of pistachios, then transfer to a serving dish. Garnish with remaining pistachios and a dusting of cinnamon. Serve warm or chilled.

Petits Soufflés

These soufflés are delicious served alone or with a praline-flavored ice cream or gelato.

1½ cups (12 fl oz/375 ml) milk

⅓ cup (3 oz/90 g) plus 3 tablespoons sugar

¼ cup (1½ oz/45 g) all-purpose (plain) flour

6 eggs, separated

¼ cup (2 fl oz/60 ml) mirabelle eau de vie or another fruit eau de vie

finely grated zest of 2 lemons

SERVES 6

1 In a heavy saucepan, heat milk over medium-high heat until bubbles appear around edge of pan. Set aside. In a large, heatproof bowl, whisk together ⅓ cup sugar and flour. Add egg yolks and whisk until mixture is smooth and lemon colored. Whisk in hot milk. Return to saucepan, reduce heat to medium-low, and whisk constantly until mixture comes to a boil. Remove from heat and stir in eau de vie and lemon zest.

2 Preheat oven to 475°F (245°C). Butter and sugar six 1-cup (8–fl oz/250-ml) ovenproof tea cups or ramekins.

3 Whip egg whites until stiff. Add 3 tablespoons sugar and continue beating until glossy.

4 Stir one-fourth of egg whites into warm milk mixture. Gently fold this mixture into remaining egg whites until just incorporated. Divide mixture evenly between prepared cups and bake until puffed and brown, 5–7 minutes. Serve immediately.

Almond Creamed Rice

Serve this sweetened porridge hot at the beginning of a meal to blunt winter-sharpened appetites. Or serve it chilled as a dessert, with more cream and a warm berry sauce. Either way, children look forward to finding an almond or two, a symbol of good luck for the coming year.

⅛ teaspoon salt

1 cup (7 oz/220 g) short-grain white rice

2½ cups (20 fl oz/625 ml) milk

2½ cups (20 fl oz/625 ml) heavy (double) cream

1 tablespoon unsalted butter, cut into pieces

1 tablespoon ground blanched almonds

1 strip lemon zest, about ½ inch (12 mm) wide and 3 inches (7.5 cm) long

1 cinnamon stick

3 tablespoons granulated sugar, or more to taste

6–8 whole blanched almonds, lightly toasted

ACCOMPANIMENTS

brown sugar

ground cinnamon

heavy (double) cream

SERVES 6–8

1 In a large, heavy saucepan, combine 1 cup (8 fl oz/250 ml) water and salt. Bring to a boil over medium-high heat. Stir in rice and cook uncovered until water returns to a boil. Reduce heat to low and simmer, stirring occasionally and watching carefully to avoid burning, until water is absorbed, 5–10 minutes.

2 Stir in milk, cream, butter, and ground almonds. Raise heat to medium and bring to a boil. Stir in lemon zest and cinnamon stick.

3 Reduce heat to low and simmer, stirring occasionally, until rice is tender and mixture has thickened, about 30 minutes. Discard lemon zest and cinnamon stick. Stir in granulated sugar. Taste, adding more sugar if desired. Stir in whole almonds.

4 Ladle into individual bowls to serve warm, or turn into a large bowl and refrigerate, covered, until serving time. (Mixture will thicken as it cools.) Top each serving with brown sugar and cinnamon and serve with a small pitcher of cream.

Praline Ile Flottante

Pralines are caramelized almonds. Use a 2-quart (2-l) charlotte pan or a straight-sided, ovenproof saucepan.

CUSTARD

2 cups (16 fl oz/500 ml) milk

6 egg yolks

¾ cup (6 oz/185 g) sugar

½ vanilla bean, split crosswise

CARAMEL

⅔ cup (5 oz/155 g) sugar

juice of ½ lemon

MERINGUE

8 egg whites, at room temperature

⅛ teaspoon salt

¼ teaspoon cream of tartar

1 cup (8 oz/250 g) sugar

⅓ cup (1½ oz/45 g) chopped pralines

SERVES 8

1 FOR CUSTARD: In a saucepan, heat milk over medium heat until bubbles appear around edge of pan. Keep hot.

2 In bowl of a stand mixer, beat egg yolks and sugar until thick and light colored. Gradually beat in hot milk. Return to saucepan with vanilla bean. Cook over low heat, stirring constantly until custard coats back of spoon, about 15 minutes. Do not let boil. Stir off heat for 1 minute to let cool, then strain through a fine-mesh sieve into a bowl. Cover with plastic wrap pressed directly on surface of custard. Let cool completely, then refrigerate.

3 FOR CARAMEL: In a small saucepan, preferably unlined copper, combine sugar, ⅓ cup (3 fl oz/80 ml) water, and lemon juice over medium heat, tilting pan to swirl contents (do not stir, as this can cause sugar to crystallize). Watch carefully; mixture will start to boil in 4–5 minutes. Continue cooking until sugar turns deep gold, about 330–335°F (165–168°C) on a candy thermometer.

4 Immediately pour in enough caramel to generously coat bottom of charlotte mold, tilting it to make an even coating.

5 To make caramel sauce for serving, add ⅓ cup (3 fl oz/80 ml) water to caramel remaining in pan and simmer, stirring, until incorporated. Set aside in a small bowl.

6 FOR MERINGUE: Preheat oven to 250°F (120°C).

7 In bowl of a stand mixer, beat egg whites on medium-low until frothy. Beat in salt and cream of tartar. Increase speed to high and gradually add sugar. Beat until whites are smooth and glossy, about 3 minutes. Fold in chopped pralines.

8 Spoon meringue into charlotte mold, gently pushing mixture against sides and smoothing top with a spatula. Bake until meringue has colored slightly and risen about ½ inch (12 mm), about 25 minutes. Let cool for 30 minutes, then refrigerate for at least 1 hour. Meringue will shrink away from sides of mold as it cools.

9 Just before serving, pour custard into serving bowl. Carefully invert meringue onto serving platter. Spoon caramel sauce around and down sides. Serve custard in small bowls, topped with wedges of meringue.

Crema Catalana

6 egg yolks

¾ cup (6 oz/185 g) plus
3 tablespoons sugar

2½ cups (20 fl oz/625 ml)
milk

1 lemon

1 cinnamon stick

3 tablespoons cornstarch
(cornflour)

SERVES 8

In Catalonia, a special small round iron plate heated red-hot over a gas flame is touched to the sugar topping to make the caramel crust on this dessert. You can caramelize the sugar under the broiler (grill) or with a small butane kitchen torch.

1 In a bowl, whisk egg yolks and ¾ cup sugar just until blended.

2 Place 2 cups (16 fl oz/500 ml) milk in a saucepan. With a vegetable peeler, pare zest off lemon in large strips, working over saucepan to catch fine spray of lemon oil. Let strips fall into milk. Add cinnamon stick. Transfer to stove top and bring to a boil over medium heat. Remove from heat and strain into egg mixture, whisking constantly.

3 In a bowl, dissolve cornstarch in remaining ½ cup milk. Stir into egg mixture. Return to saucepan. Cook over low heat, stirring, just until it bubbles and thickens, about 1 minute. Remove from heat. Divide among 8 ramekins. Let cool. Cover and refrigerate for at least 2 hours or overnight.

4 Preheat broiler (grill). Sprinkle remaining 3 tablespoons sugar evenly over custards. Broil (grill) 4 inches (10 cm) from heat until top is caramelized, about 2 minutes.

cookies & cakes

Cakes and cookies hold a place of honor in the traditional lexicon of desserts. Birthdays are celebrated with cake, dinner parties are topped off with a torte, and after school, cookies reign supreme. An element of ceremony and a certain joy are associated with cutting a thick slice, unwrapping a cupcake, deconstructing the layers, sampling the frosting, breaking a cookie, and practicing the ancient art of dunking.

Easter Ring Cookies

In Italy, *taralli* can be prepared as either sweet cookies or savory biscuits. The savory version is often flavored with pepper or fennel and is served with red wine. Here, the sweet version is glazed with a sweet lemon icing. Taralli keep well in a plastic container with a tight-fitting lid. To add a little color, sprinkle with multicolored nonpareils.

DOUGH

5½ cups (27½ oz/860 g) all-purpose (plain) flour

1½ tablespoons baking powder

6 eggs

1 cup (8 oz/250 g) granulated sugar

¾ cup (6 oz/185 g) unsalted butter, melted

1½ tablespoons vanilla extract (essence)

ICING

3 cups (12 oz/375 g) confectioners' (icing) sugar

1 tablespoon fresh lemon juice

1 teaspoon vanilla extract (essence)

MAKES 16 LARGE COOKIES

1 FOR DOUGH: Preheat oven to 350°F (180°C). Line 3 baking sheets with parchment (baking) paper. Combine flour and baking powder, mixing well.

2 In a bowl, whisk eggs to blend, then whisk in granulated sugar, melted butter, and vanilla. Fold in flour mixture.

3 Turn dough out onto a floured surface and knead lightly to mix. Separate into 16 equal pieces. Roll each into an 8-inch (20-cm) rope, then form into a circle. Place on prepared baking sheets.

4 Bake cookies until deep golden, 30 to 35 minutes. Let cool on wire racks.

5 FOR ICING: In a saucepan, combine confectioners' sugar, lemon juice, and vanilla. Stir in ¼ cup (2 fl oz/60 ml) water. Cook over low heat until lukewarm. Brush over tops of cookies.

Rhubarb Pound Cake

The tangy flavor of rhubarb complements the buttery richness of pound cake. To make this cake successfully, butter and eggs must be at room temperature.

½ lb (250 g) rhubarb, cut into ¼-inch (6-mm) pieces, about 2 cups

1¼ cups (10 oz/315 g) sugar

1¾ cups (9 oz/280 g) all-purpose (plain) flour

¼ teaspoon salt

1 teaspoon baking powder

¾ cup (6 oz/185 g) unsalted butter, softened

3 eggs, at room temperature

1½ teaspoons vanilla extract (essence)

SERVES 8–10

1 In a small saucepan, combine rhubarb and ¼ cup (2 oz/60 g) sugar. Cover and cook over very low heat until rhubarb is tender, but not falling apart, about 10 minutes. Stir occasionally to prevent burning. Drain, discarding the liquid. Set aside and let cool to room temperature.

2 Preheat oven to 350°F (180°C). Generously butter a 9-by-5-inch (23-by-13-cm) loaf pan. Sift flour, salt, and baking powder together in a bowl.

3 In a stand mixer fitted with paddle attachment, beat butter until creamy. Add remaining 1 cup (8 oz/250 g) sugar and beat until light and fluffy.

4 In a bowl, whisk eggs and vanilla together. With mixer on medium speed, pour eggs into butter mixture in a very fine stream, stopping occasionally.

If mixture starts to appear curdled while eggs are being added, add 1 or 2 tablespoons of flour mixture. On low speed, add flour mixture. Using a rubber spatula, fold in cooled rhubarb.

5 Pour batter into prepared pan. Smooth with a spatula and make a lengthwise slit 1 inch (2.5 cm) deep to minimize splitting.

6 Bake until cake is browned and a skewer inserted in its center comes out clean, about 1 hour and 10 minutes. Let cool in pan for 2 minutes. Unmold and let cool right side up on a wire rack.

Buzzy Bees

A variation on classic pinwheel cookies, these chocolate and vanilla treats are irresistible. Kids will love eating them stripe by stripe.

½ cup (4 oz/125 g) unsalted butter, softened

½ cup (4 oz/125 g) sugar

1 egg

½ teaspoon vanilla extract (essence)

1½ cups (7½ oz/235 g) all-purpose (plain) flour

½ teaspoon baking powder

¼ teaspoon salt

1½ oz (45 g) semisweet (plain) chocolate

MAKES ABOUT 5 DOZEN COOKIES

1 In a bowl, use an electric mixer to cream butter and sugar until light. Add egg and vanilla and mix to combine. In another bowl, combine flour, baking powder, and salt. Add dry ingredients gradually to first bowl and mix until incorporated.

2 In top of a double boiler over barely simmering water, melt chocolate. Let cool slightly.

3 Divide dough in half, leaving half in bowl and placing other half between 2 pieces of parchment (baking) paper. Roll out vanilla dough into an 8-by-6-inch (20-by-15-cm) rectangle, ¼ inch (6 mm) thick. Place on a baking sheet and cover with plastic wrap. Stir melted chocolate into remaining dough in bowl. Repeat rolling process with chocolate dough. Refrigerate both doughs for 1 hour.

4 Carefully remove top piece of parchment from both doughs, and invert exposed chocolate dough onto vanilla dough. Refrigerate for 15 minutes. Using a sharp knife, trim stacked dough into an even 8-by-6-inch (20-by-15-cm) rectangle.

5 Slice dough lengthwise into 3 strips, each 2 inches (5 cm) wide. Place each dough strip on top of next, to create 6 alternating stripes of vanilla and chocolate in an even block. Wrap and refrigerate for 30 minutes.

6 Preheat oven to 350°F (180°C). Line a baking sheet with parchment (baking) paper or use a nonstick baking sheet. Cut dough crosswise into slices ⅛ inch (3 mm) thick. Place on prepared baking sheet.

7 Bake cookies until just beginning to turn golden brown, 7–10 minutes. Let cool slightly on baking sheet. Transfer to a wire rack to cool completely.

Spritz with Sprinkles

2 cups (1 lb/500 g) unsalted butter, softened

1 cup (8 oz/250 g) sugar

1 egg

1 teaspoon vanilla extract (essence)

4 cups (1¼ lb/625 g) all-purpose (plain) flour

¼ teaspoon salt

8 oz (250 g) white chocolate

sprinkles, for decorating

MAKES ABOUT 7 DOZEN COOKIES

Traditionally, these cookies are shaped into rings using a cookie press, which is available at cookware stores.

1 Preheat over then 400°F (200°C).

2 In a bowl, cream butter and sugar together until fluffy. Stir in egg and vanilla.

3 In another bowl, combine flour and salt. Add flour mixture to butter mixture in 4 batches, mixing after each addition.

4 Roll the stiff dough on a lightly floured surface into a cylinder and fill a cookie press fitted with the single-hole star attachment. Carefully press out cookie dough onto a nonstick baking sheet to make a strip of dough 3-4 inches (7.5-10 cm) long. Cut dough off with a knife. Shape strips into circles, placing them about 2 inches (5 cm) apart. Bake cookies until light brown on the bottom, 8-10 minutes. Cool on a wire rack.

5 Meanwhile, in a double boiler, melt white chocolate. Brush a thin layer of chocolate on the bottom half of each cooled cookie and dip into sprinkles.

Boston Cream Pie

2½ cups (12½ oz/390 g)
all-purpose (plain) flour

3 ½ teaspoons baking powder

½ teaspoon salt

6 tablespoons (3 oz/90 g)
unsalted butter, softened

1⅔ cups (13 oz/410 g) sugar

2 teaspoons vanilla extract
(essence)

1 cup (8 fl oz/250 ml) milk

3 eggs

PASTRY CREAM AND GLAZE

9 egg yolks

1½ cups (12 oz/375 g) sugar

large pinch of salt

¼ cup (1 oz/30 g)
cornstarch (cornflour)

1 vanilla bean

2 ½ cups (20 fl oz/625 ml) milk

¼ cup (2 fl oz/60 ml)
heavy (double) cream

½ cup (1½ oz/45 g) cocoa powder

1½ teaspoons powdered gelatin

SERVES 8–10

1 Preheat oven to 350°F (180°C). Spray a 9-inch (23-cm) round, 3-inch (7.5-cm) deep cake pan with nonstick spray. Line bottom with parchment (baking) paper. Sift together flour, baking powder, and salt. Set aside.

2 In bowl of a stand mixer fitted with paddle attachment, cream butter and sugar on medium-high speed until light. Reduce speed to low. Stir vanilla into milk. Add flour and milk mixtures to butter and sugar alternately in 3 additions, mixing well and scraping down bowl after each addition. On medium speed, add eggs one at a time, beating well after each addition.

3 Spread batter in prepared pan. Bake until a wooden skewer inserted into center comes out clean, about 1 hour. Let cool in pan for 10 minutes. Run a knife around inside edge of pan and invert onto a wire rack. Peel off parchment and let cool completely.

4 FOR PASTRY CREAM AND GLAZE: In a bowl, whisk together egg yolks, ½ cup (4 oz/125 g) sugar, and salt. Whisk in cornstarch. Set aside. Cut vanilla bean in half lengthwise and scrape out seeds. In a heavy saucepan, combine vanilla bean, seeds, and milk. Cook over medium-high heat until milk bubbles around edges.

Slowly pour milk mixture into egg mixture, whisking constantly. Return mixture to pan. Over medium-low heat, cook, stirring constantly, until as thick as mayonnaise, 5–7 minutes. Remove from heat, strain into a clean bowl, and discard vanilla bean. Cover with plastic wrap pressed directly on surface of pastry cream. Let cool completely and then refrigerate.

5 In a saucepan, stir together cream, remaining 1 cup (8 oz/250 g) sugar, ¾ cup (6 fl oz/180 ml) water, and cocoa powder. Bring to a boil, whisking often, then reduce heat to low and simmer, stirring often, until it thickly coats back of a spoon, 10–12 minutes. Remove from heat and pour into a bowl. While glaze cools, stir gelatin into 1 tablespoon water in a small bowl and let sit for 2 minutes, then place over a small saucepan of barely simmering water, stirring until liquid and translucent. Whisk into glaze. Refrigerate, stirring occasionally, until glaze is a thick pouring consistency, 30–60 minutes.

6 Cut cake in half horizontally. Place bottom half on a rimmed plate, spread with pastry cream, top with second layer, and press gently. Drizzle glaze over top of cake, letting it drip down sides. Refrigerate. Let sit at room temperature for 20 minutes before serving.

Cappuccino Cheesecake

The base for this decadent cheesecake is like a brownie. To save a step and make a crisper crust, crush chocolate wafers, add enough melted butter so the crumbs hold together, then press into the pan and bake as directed.

1 cup (8 oz/250 g) cold unsalted butter, cut into small pieces, plus ½ cup (4 oz/125 g) unsalted butter, softened

1½ cups (12 oz/375 g) granulated sugar

1¼ cups (6½ oz/200 g) all-purpose (plain) flour

¼ cup (1½ oz/45 g) rice flour

½ cup (1½ oz/45 g) cocoa powder, plus more for dusting

large pinch of salt

1½ lb (750 g) cream cheese, softened

4 eggs

2 cups (16 oz/500 g) sour cream

2 tablespoons instant espresso powder, preferably Medaglia d'Oro

½ cup (3½ oz/105 g) firmly packed dark brown sugar

¼ cup (2 fl oz/60 ml) heavy (double) cream

SERVES 8–10

1 In bowl of a stand mixer fitted with paddle attachment, combine 1 cup cold butter pieces, ½ cup (4 oz/125 g) granulated sugar, flours, cocoa powder, and salt. Mix on low speed until dough comes together. Roll dough into a 9-inch (23-cm) circle and pat into bottom of a 9-inch (23-cm) springform pan. Refrigerate for at least 30 minutes or up to overnight.

2 Preheat oven to 300°F (150°C). Bake crust for 30 minutes. Let cool completely.

3 In bowl of a stand mixer fitted with paddle attachment, beat cream cheese on medium speed until smooth. Add remaining 1 cup (8 oz/250 g) granulated sugar and beat until smooth. Add eggs one at a time, beating well after each addition. Stir in sour cream and espresso powder. Mix until smooth.

4 Pour filling into crust and spread evenly. Place pan in a large roasting or baking pan, then place in oven. Carefully fill roasting pan halfway up side of springform pan with hot water. Bake until cheesecake looks set from center to edges, but not dry, when pan is gently shaken, 1¼–1½ hours.

5 Remove from oven and let cool at room temperature for 30 minutes. Refrigerate until chilled throughout, about 1 hour.

6 In a small, heavy saucepan, combine brown sugar, remaining ½ cup butter, and cream over low heat until sugar is dissolved. Raise heat to high and bring to a boil. Reduce heat to medium and cook, stirring constantly, until thick and smooth. Let cool to room temperature.

7 When ready to serve, remove cheesecake from refrigerator and transfer to a large serving plate. Cut with a hot, dry knife. Serve slices drizzled with caramel glaze and dusted with cocoa powder.

Marbled Chocolate Meringues

Drizzling melted chocolate into the beaten egg whites creates strikingly marbled meringues. Even with chocolate, the cookies are feather light.

3 oz (90 g) bittersweet chocolate, chopped

4 egg whites

1 cup (8 oz/250 g) sugar

MAKES 20 COOKIES

1 Preheat oven to 275°F (135°C). Line 2 baking sheets with parchment (baking) paper.

2 In a saucepan, bring 1–2 inches (2.5–5 cm) water to a simmer. Put chocolate in a heatproof bowl over (but not touching) simmering water and melt, stirring occasionally. Set aside and let cool slightly.

3 In another heatproof bowl, combine egg whites and sugar over (but not touching) simmering water and whisk until mixture is hot, 4–5 minutes. Remove bowl from heat. Using an electric mixer, beat on high speed until stiff peaks form and mixture is lukewarm, 4–5 minutes.

4 Drizzle melted chocolate over egg white mixture, folding in with a rubber spatula until just marbled.

5 With a soup spoon, drop batter in large mounds spaced 1½–2 inches (4–5 cm) apart on prepared baking sheets. Bake until crisp outside and still chewy inside, 35–40 minutes. Transfer sheets to a wire rack and let cool completely before removing cookies from parchment. Store in an airtight container.

Orange-Almond Cake
with Honey Syrup

Orange-blossom honey is an obvious choice, but any lightly-flavored honey is a suitable substitute. This dessert is lovely with whipped cream.

1 organic navel orange, unpeeled, scrubbed, and cut into ½-inch (12-mm) chunks

¾ cup (3 oz/90 g) whole blanched almonds

1 cup (6 oz/185 g) raisins (plumped in warm water if hard, and squeezed dry)

½ cup (4 oz/125 g) unsalted butter, softened

½ cup (4 oz/125 g) sugar

2 tablespoons plus ¼ cup (3 oz/90 ml) orange-blossom honey

2 eggs, at room temperature

¼ teaspoon almond extract (essence)

2 cups (10 oz/315 g) unbleached all-purpose (plain) flour

2 teaspoons baking powder

½ teaspoon salt

1 teaspoon orange flower water

SERVES 8-10

1 Preheat oven to 325°F (165°C). Lightly butter an 8-inch (20-cm) springform pan and line bottom with parchment (baking) paper. Butter parchment and flour pan.

2 In a food processor, pulse orange chunks, almonds, and raisins to a rough paste.

3 In a large bowl, cream butter with sugar and 2 tablespoons honey until light and smooth. Add eggs one at a time, beating well after each addition. Mix in fruit-and-nut mixture along with almond extract. In a separate bowl, combine flour, baking powder, and salt. Stir into butter mixture ½ cup (4 oz/125 g) at a time.

4 Spread batter evenly in prepared pan; lightly rap on the counter. Bake until top is browned and springs back when gently pressed, about 1¼ hours.

5 Transfer to a wire rack and let cool for 10 minutes. Invert cake onto a serving plate and peel off parchment.

6 In a saucepan, combine ¼ cup honey, 1 tablespoon water, and orange flower water and boil over medium-high heat for 30 seconds, stirring constantly. Brush hot syrup over top and sides of warm cake, allowing it to seep in, until all syrup is used.

Twice-Baked Almond Cookies

These fantastic cookies, studded with crunchy whole almonds, are similar to Italian biscotti. Serve alongside a strong cup of coffee.

2 cups (10 oz/315 g) all-purpose (plain) flour

⅔ cup (5 oz/155 g) sugar

1½ teaspoons baking powder

¼ teaspoon salt

1 tablespoon grated lemon zest

5 tablespoons (2½ oz/75 g) cold unsalted butter, cut into bits

2 eggs

½ teaspoon vanilla extract (essence)

1 teaspoon almond extract (essence)

1 cup (5½ oz/170 g) whole almonds

MAKES 3 DOZEN COOKIES

1 Preheat oven to 350°F (180°C). Line a baking sheet with parchment (baking) paper.

2 In a food processor, combine flour, sugar, baking powder, salt, and lemon zest. Add butter and pulse until mixture resembles coarse meal. Add eggs and vanilla and almond extracts. Pulse just to blend. Transfer to a bowl. Lightly knead in almonds.

3 Transfer dough to a lightly floured surface and divide in half. Shape each half into a 10-inch (25-cm) log about 1½ inches (4 cm) wide. Place logs 3 inches (7.5 cm) apart on prepared baking sheet.

4 Bake until logs begin to turn golden, about 25 minutes. Remove from oven and let cool to touch on a wire rack.

5 Raise oven temperature to 400°F (200°C). Transfer logs to a cutting board. Using a very sharp chef's knife, cut each log into 18 equal slices. Lay slices cut side down on same baking sheet and bake for 7 minutes. Turn oven off and turn cookies over. Return to oven until golden and crisp, 10–15 minutes. When cool, store in an airtight container.

Chocolate Mousse Cake

CHOCOLATE SPONGE CAKE

⅔ cup (3 oz/90 g) sifted
all-purpose (plain) flour

⅓ cup (1 oz/30 g) cocoa powder

¼ teaspoon salt

6 large eggs, at room temperature

1 tablespoon vanilla extract
(essence)

1 cup (8 oz/250 g) sugar

CHOCOLATE MOUSSE

6 oz (185 g) bittersweet chocolate,
chopped

3 tablespoons unsalted butter

2 tablespoons dark rum

1 teaspoon vanilla extract (essence)

1½ teaspoons unflavored gelatin

3 large eggs, at room temperature,
separated

3 tablespoons plus ¼ cup
(2 oz/60 g) sugar

¼ teaspoon cream of tartar

½ cup (4 fl oz/125 ml) heavy
(double) cream, chilled

chocolate curls, for garnish

SERVES 8–10

The suitable end to a decadent dinner—or the rich reward for a light one—is rich, rum-infused chocolate mousse layered with chocolate sponge cake.

1 FOR SPONGE CAKE: Preheat oven to 350°F (180°C). Line an 18-by-13-inch (45-by-33-cm) rimmed baking sheet with parchment (baking) paper and set aside.

2 In a bowl, sift together flour, cocoa powder, and salt; set aside. In another bowl, combine eggs and vanilla. Using an electric mixer, beat on high speed until light and pale yellow, about 10 minutes. Slowly add sugar and continue to beat for 2–3 minutes. Sift one-fourth of flour mixture over egg mixture and fold in. Repeat 3 more times with remaining flour mixture. Pour batter into prepared pan and spread evenly. Bake until a wooden skewer inserted into center comes out clean, 25–30 minutes. Let pan cool completely on a wire rack.

3 FOR MOUSSE: In top of a double-boiler, combine chocolate, butter, rum, and vanilla and stir until melted and blended. Transfer to a small bowl and set aside. Meanwhile, in another small bowl, sprinkle gelatin over 3 tablespoons water and let stand for 5 minutes to soften.

4 In clean double boiler, combine egg yolks, gelatin mixture, and 3 tablespoons sugar and whisk constantly until thick and pale yellow, 6–7 minutes. Remove from heat and whisk into melted chocolate mixture. Set aside and let cool.

5 In a bowl, beat egg whites with an electric mixer on medium-high speed until soft peaks form. Beat in cream of tartar. Gradually add remaining ¼ cup (2 oz/60 g) sugar. Increase to high speed and continue beating until peaks are stiff. Stir one-third of beaten egg whites into cooled chocolate mixture. Fold in remaining whites. In a clean bowl, beat cream on medium-high speed until soft peaks form. Fold cream into chocolate mixture.

6 To assemble, turn cooled cake out onto cutting board, peel off parchment, and cut into 4 equal-sized rectangles. Turn 1 rectangle upside down and place on serving plate. Spread with one quarter of the mousse and top with another rectangle of cake. Repeat, alternating layers, ending with mousse. Refrigerate for at least 4 hours or up to overnight. Trim cake sides to reveal layers. Garnish with chocolate.

Dutch Shortbread

1²⁄₃ cups (8 oz/250 g)
all-purpose (plain) flour

½ cup (3½ oz/105 g) firmly
packed light brown sugar

1 teaspoon ground cardamom

1 teaspoon ground cinnamon

½ teaspoon ground cloves

¾ cup (6 oz/185 g) cold unsalted
butter, cut into small pieces

1 egg, lightly beaten

MAKES 2–6 MOLDED FIGURES OR
ABOUT 3 DOZEN 2-INCH (5-CM) COOKIES

These cardamom-spiced shortbread cookies are traditionally formed by pressing the dough into decorative wooden molds that can range anywhere from 6 to 12 inches (15 to 30 cm) in length. Once given shape, the dough is inverted onto a baking sheet, ready for the oven. The same dough can be formed into a cylinder and sliced into rounds for baking.

1 In a food processor, combine flour, brown sugar, cardamom, cinnamon, and cloves. Pulse to blend. Add butter and pulse until mixture resembles fine bread crumbs. Add egg and process just until dough begins to form a ball.

2 For large molded cookies, turn dough out onto a floured work surface and, with floured hands, form into a flattened disk. For sliced cookies, divide dough into 2 equal portions. Form each into a 2-inch (5-cm) thick cylinder about 7 inches (18 cm) long. Wrap in plastic and refrigerate until firm, at least 2 hours or up to 2 days.

3 Preheat oven to 350°F (180°C). Butter a baking sheet or line with parchment (baking) paper.

4 Dust molds with flour, tapping out excess. Divide dough into pieces roughly the shape and size of each mold. Press dough into the molds and invert onto the baking sheet, spacing at least 1 inch (2.5 cm) apart. For round cookies, slice cylinders of dough into pieces about ³⁄₈ inch (1 cm) thick.

5 Bake until set and golden brown at edges, 10–12 minutes for sliced cookies or 15–20 minutes for most molded cookies. If molded cookies are not completely baked after 20 minutes, reduce oven temperature to 325°F (165°C) and continue baking until done. (Cookies will firm and crisp as they cool.) Let cool on baking sheet for 5 minutes, then transfer to a wire rack to cool completely. Store in an airtight container.

Dutch Letter Cookies

On December 6, St. Nicholas Day, children receive spicy cookies shaped in letters to match their own initials. Decorate with silver dragees, or divide icing into small bowls and color with 1 or 2 drops of food coloring.

½ cup (4 oz/125 g) unsalted butter, softened

1 cup (7 oz/220 g) superfine (caster) sugar

⅓ cup (3½ 105 g) unsulfured molasses

1 egg

2½ cups (12½ oz/390 g) all-purpose (plain) flour

2 teaspoons baking powder

1 teaspoon ground cinnamon

1 teaspoon ground ginger

½ teaspoon ground cloves

¼ teaspoon finely ground black pepper

2 teaspoons finely grated lemon zest

ICING

3 tablespoons meringue powder

4 cups (1 lb/500 g) confectioner's (icing) sugar, sifted

silver dragees (optional)

MAKES ABOUT 2½ DOZEN
3-INCH (7.5-CM) COOKIES

1 In a large bowl, use an electric mixer to cream butter until fluffy and light. Add superfine sugar and beat until mixture no longer feels gritty. Gradually beat in molasses on low speed. Add egg and beat on low speed until blended.

2 Sift flour, baking powder, cinnamon, ginger, cloves, and pepper onto a sheet of waxed paper. Add to butter mixture in thirds, mixing on low speed after each addition until well blended. Mix in lemon zest. Turn out onto a floured work surface and divide dough into 2 equal portions. Form each into a flattened disk, wrap in plastic wrap, and refrigerate until firm, at least overnight or up to 2 days.

3 Preheat oven to 350°F (180°C). Lightly grease 2 baking sheets or line with parchment paper. Roll out 1 chilled dough disk between 2 sheets of lightly floured parchment paper until about ⅛ inch (3 mm).

4 Using 3-inch (7.5-cm) alphabet or other cookie cutters, cut out shapes. Using a thin offset spatula, carefully transfer to prepared baking sheets, placing cookies about 1 inch (2.5 cm) apart. Repeat with remaining dough disk, then gather up scraps, reroll, and cut out additional cookies.

5 Bake cookies until just set, about 10 minutes. (Cookies will firm as they cool.) Let cool on pans for 5–10 minutes. Transfer to wire racks to cool completely before decorating.

6 FOR ICING: In a large bowl, use an electric mixer on medium speed to combine meringue powder and 6 tablespoons (3 fl oz/90 ml) warm water. On low speed, gradually beat in confectioners' sugar until blended, then beat on high speed until thick and smooth, about 5 minutes. Beat in more warm water, a teaspoon at a time, if icing is too thick.

7 Pipe or spread icing onto cookies. Decorate with silver dragees, if desired. Let icing set completely, 1–3 hours. Store in an airtight container.

Norwegian Celebration Cake

1½ cups (8 oz/250 g) whole almonds

1½ cups (8 oz/250 g) whole blanched almonds

4 cups (1 lb/500 g) confectioners' (icing) sugar

3 tablespoons all-purpose (plain) flour

1 teaspoon ground cinnamon

3 egg whites, at room temperature

GLAZE

¼ cup (2 fl oz/60 ml) fresh orange or lemon juice, milk, or water, or more if needed

1 cup (4 oz/125 g) confectioners' (icing) sugar, sifted

2 teaspoons finely grated orange or lemon zest (optional)

silver dragees (optional)

SERVES 12 OR MORE

Norway's *kransekake* is a pyramid of chewy almond-meringue rings, whimsically decorated like an edible Christmas tree. Serve with ice cream or whipped cream flavored with orange zest and brandy. This popular cake is often baked for weddings and birthdays, as well as at Christmas.

1 Preheat oven to 400°F (200°C). Line 3 baking sheets with parchment (baking) paper.

2 In a food processor or blender, grind nuts to a rough powder and transfer to a large bowl. Add confectioners' sugar, flour, and cinnamon, stirring to blend well.

3 With an electric mixer, whisk egg whites on high speed until soft peaks form. Stir whites into nut mixture until well blended. Turn mixture onto a lightly floured surface and knead thoroughly to form a soft, workable dough.

4 Divide dough into 3 portions. Roll each portion into a rope about ½ inch (12 mm) thick. Cut ropes into 18 pieces of increasing length, beginning with 5 inches (13 cm) long and adding just under 1 inch (2.5 cm) to the next; the final rope should be about 20 inches (50 cm) long. Form each piece into a ring, pressing ends together to seal and smoothing joint with a damp finger. Place 5-inch (13-cm) ring in center of first baking sheet; 6-inch (15-cm) ring on second, and so on, so rings on each baking sheet are arranged in concentric circles, but not touching. (First baking sheet should have rings 1, 4, 7, 10, 13, 16; second sheet should have rings 2, 5, etc.)

5 Bake until rings are barely golden and set but not firm (still a little chewy in center), 8–10 minutes. Let cool on baking sheets for 5 minutes, then carefully transfer to wire racks, peeling off parchment paper as needed. Cool completely.

6 To assemble, place largest ring on a serving platter. Top with next largest ring and repeat with remaining rings to form a pyramid.

7 FOR GLAZE: In a bowl, whisk liquid into confectioners' sugar until well blended. Stir in citrus zest. If icing is too thick, stir in more liquid, a few drops at a time. Drizzle *kransekake* with glaze. Decorate with silver dragees, if desired.

8 To serve, carefully lift off a stack of upper rings so part of pyramid remains intact. Cut or break bottom rings into serving pieces.

Angel Food Cake
with Fresh Berries

Orange flower water is available at specialty food stores. Vanilla extract (essence) can be substituted, although the resulting cake will lack the delicate floral-citrus flavor.

MIXED BERRIES

3 cups (12 oz/375 g) mixed fresh berries, such as blueberries, blackberries, and quartered strawberries

2 tablespoons granulated sugar

ANGEL FOOD CAKE

1½ cups (12 fl oz/375 ml) egg whites (10 to 12)

1 cup (3 oz/90g) sifted cake flour

1¼ cups (10 oz/315 g) granulated sugar

2 teaspoons orange flower water

1 teaspoon cream of tartar

½ teaspoon salt

confectioners' (icing) sugar, for dusting

coconut or vanilla ice cream, for serving

SERVES 8-10

1 FOR MIXED BERRIES: In a large bowl, toss berries with granulated sugar. Let stand at room temperature for at least 30 minutes or up to 2 hours.

2 FOR ANGEL FOOD CAKE: Position a rack in lower third of oven and preheat to 375°F (190°C).

3 Sift flour and ¼ cup (2 oz/60 g) granulated sugar into a bowl or onto a sheet of waxed paper. Sift two more times.

4 In bowl of a stand mixer, beat egg whites on medium speed until frothy. Add orange flower water, cream of tartar, and salt. Increase speed to medium-high and beat just until soft peaks begin to form. Gradually beat in remaining granulated sugar, 2 tablespoons at a time, occasionally scraping down side of bowl. Increase mixer speed to high and beat until stiff, glossy peaks form. Be careful not to over-beat. Sprinkle flour mixture over whites in thirds, beating on low speed just until blended with each addition.

5 Gently pour batter into an ungreased 10-inch (25-cm) tube pan. Run a rubber spatula or long knife through batter to eliminate any large air bubbles and smooth top.

6 Bake until top of cake is golden and a cake tester comes out clean, about 40 minutes. Remove cake from oven and immediately invert pan over neck of a bottle. Leave inverted over bottle until cake is completely cool. Turn pan right side up. Run a long, thin knife smoothly around outer edge of pan and center tube. Remove outer rim of pan and run knife under bottom of cake. Invert to release cake from tube, and invert again onto a serving plate. (Cake may be made a day ahead and kept, covered, at room temperature.)

7 Just before serving, dust cake with confectioners' sugar. Serve with mixed berries and scoops of coconut or vanilla ice cream.

Chestnut Roulade

4 eggs, at room temperature

⅓ cup (3 oz/90 g) plus
1 tablespoon granulated sugar

¼ cup (1 oz/30 g) cake
(soft-wheat) flour, sifted

CHESTNUT WHIPPED CREAM
1 cup (8 fl oz/250 ml) heavy
(double) cream

½ cup (5 oz/155 g) sweetened
chestnut purée

confectioners' (icing) sugar,
for dusting

Chestnuts in Syrup or
marrons glacés, for garnish

SERVES 12–14

Look for sweetened chestnut purée, chestnuts in syrup, and *marrons glacés* in well-stocked markets and specialty food stores.

1 Preheat oven to 475°F (245°C). Line an 18-by-12½-inch (45-by-32-cm) rimmed baking sheet with parchment (baking) paper and butter sides.

2 Separate 2 eggs, setting whites aside. In bowl of a stand mixer fitted with whisk attachment, combine 2 egg yolks and 2 whole eggs. Beat at medium speed, gradually adding ⅓ cup granulated sugar. Increase speed to high and beat until egg mixture is thick, pale, and almost doubled in volume. Transfer to another bowl.

3 Wash and dry bowl and whisk. In bowl, beat egg whites with whisk until foamy. Add 1 tablespoon granulated sugar. Increase speed to high and beat until soft peaks form. Fold whites into egg mixture.

4 Sift flour over egg mixture (this is a second sifting) and fold in. Pour batter onto prepared baking sheet and spread as evenly as possible. Bake for 3 minutes. Rotate sheet so cake bakes evenly and continue to bake until cake is golden, 4 minutes longer. Remove from oven.

5 Run a table knife around edges and slide out cake, still on parchment. Let cake cool, paper side down, on a wire rack. When cool, lift paper and cake and return to cooled baking sheet. Cover with plastic wrap and refrigerate until needed.

6 FOR CHESTNUT WHIPPED CREAM: In a bowl, whip cream until soft peaks form. In a small bowl, mix sweetened chestnut purée with a small amount of whipped cream, then fold mixture into whipped cream.

7 Place cake, paper side up, on another piece of parchment. Carefully peel off top piece of paper. Trim edges of cake to facilitate rolling. Spread whipped cream on cake with an icing spatula.

8 With a long side of the cake toward you, roll into a log. Transfer to a serving plate, placing seam side down. With a sharp knife, cut a diagonal piece from each end of log to form a clean edge. Dust with confectioners' sugar. Wipe plate clean with a paper towel. Garnish cake with chestnuts in syrup or marrons glacés. Refrigerate until serving.

pies & tarts

There are few smells more tempting than that of a pie baking, and few sights more tempting than that of the golden pastry emerging from the oven. Whether two crusts or one, it's all about anticipation—waiting for the first slice. If pie, particularly apple, is pure all-American comfort, then tarts are a little more exotic, a tad racier, showing off their wares rather than modestly awaiting the pie server. And once on the dessert plate, a slice of pie or a perfect tart offers a delicious contrast between crust and filling.

Tarte au Chocolat

This will be one of your most popular desserts. Refrigerating the tart for 24 hours ensures a trufflelike texture.

PASTRY

5 tablespoons (2½ oz/75 g) unsalted butter, softened

⅔ cup (3 oz/90 g) confectioners' (icing) sugar

2 egg yolks

1 cup (5 oz/155 g) plus 3 tablespoons all-purpose (plain) flour

FILLING

1¼ cups (10 fl oz/310 ml) heavy (double) cream

10½ oz (330 g) bittersweet chocolate, finely chopped

2 eggs, lightly beaten

SERVES 10-12

1 FOR PASTRY: In a food processor, combine butter, confectioners' sugar, and egg yolks. Add flour and pulse until dough just forms a ball. Shape into a disk, wrap with plastic, and refrigerate for 1 hour or overnight.

2 On a lightly floured surface, roll out dough about ⅛ inch (3 mm) thick. Line a 9½-inch (24-cm) fluted tart pan with removable bottom with dough. Using a fork, prick base. Cover with plastic wrap and refrigerate for at least 1 hour.

3 Preheat oven to 325°F (165°C). Line tart shell with aluminum foil and fill with pie weights or dried beans. Bake until firm, about 15 minutes. Remove weights and foil. Transfer to a wire rack and let cool.

4 Raise oven temperature to 400°F (200°C).

5 FOR FILLING: In a saucepan, heat cream over medium heat just until small bubbles begin to form at edges. Remove from heat, add chocolate, and stir until melted, 1–2 minutes. Whisk slowly into beaten eggs, to prevent curdling.

6 Pour mixture into tart shell and bake until crust is golden and filling is lightly set, about 15 minutes. Let cool on wire rack. Refrigerate for 24 hours before serving; cover tart with plastic wrap after about 2 hours. Serve at room temperature.

Rhubarb-Strawberry
Custard Tart

PASTRY

¾ cup (6 oz/185 g)
unsalted butter, softened

½ cup (3½ oz/105 g)
firmly packed light brown sugar

1 egg, at room temperature

½ teaspoon vanilla extract
(essence)

1¾ cups (9 oz/280 g) unbleached
all-purpose (plain) flour

pinch of salt

FILLING AND GLAZE

2 cups (8 oz/250 g) fresh
strawberries, hulled and sliced

½ pound (250 g) rhubarb,
cut into ¼-inch (6-mm) pieces,
about 2 cups

⅔ cup (5 fl oz/160 ml) heavy
(double) cream

⅓ cup (2½ oz/75 g) firmly
packed light brown sugar

2 eggs

⅓ cup (3½ oz/105 g)
apricot preserves

SERVES 8

True rhubarb fans can eliminate the strawberries and double the amount of rhubarb in this tart, in which the fruit is complemented by the faint molasses flavor of brown sugar. Put the tart pan on a baking sheet to make the transfer in and out of the oven easier.

1 FOR PASTRY: Using a stand mixer fitted with paddle attachment, beat butter on medium speed until creamy. Add brown sugar and beat until pale. Beat in egg and vanilla. On low speed, add flour and salt, and mix until just blended. Flatten dough to a disk ½ inch (12 mm) thick and wrap in plastic. Refrigerate for at least 1 hour or up to 3 days.

2 Preheat oven to 400°F (200°C). Unwrap dough and place on a lightly floured surface. If dough is very cold, beat with a rolling pin to make more malleable. Roll into a round ⅛ inch (3 mm) thick. If dough cracks when rolled, gather into a ball, knead a few times, and roll again.

3 Fit dough into a 9-inch (23-cm) round tart pan with removable bottom. Ease dough into bottom and up sides of pan, then run rolling pin over top to cut off excess. Press dough to sides of pan. Freeze tart shell for 20 minutes.

4 Line tart shell with parchment (baking) paper. Fill with pie weights or dried beans.

5 Bake until sides are lightly browned, about 10 minutes. Remove weights and parchment and bake until bottom is set, 5 minutes longer.

6 FOR FILLING AND GLAZE: Strew strawberries and rhubarb in baked tart shell. Whisk cream, brown sugar, and eggs together in a bowl. Pour over fruit, leaving a ⅛-inch (3-mm) margin at top so filling won't overflow in oven.

7 Bake until firm and well browned and a knife inserted in center comes out clean, 40–45 minutes. Let cool completely and transfer to a serving platter.

8 In a small saucepan, mix preserves with 2 tablespoons water. Heat over low heat. Push through a sieve with the back of a spoon. Brush tart with glaze and let set, about 1 hour.

Mulberry Galette

Mulberries, like raspberries, come in a few colors, but red is the color you'll find most in the eastern and southern United States. If you can't find black mulberries, substitute blackberries or boysenberries. Serve with whipped cream flavored with orange zest or orange liqueur.

PASTRY

1½ cups (7½ oz/235 g) all-purpose (plain) flour

1 tablespoon sugar

½ teaspoon salt

grated zest of 1 orange

½ cup (4 oz/125 g) plus 2 tablespoons cold unsalted butter

FILLING

4 cups (1 lb/500 g) fresh black mulberries

2–4 tablespoons sugar, plus more for sprinkling

½ teaspoon instant tapioca

2 tablespoons unsalted butter, melted

SERVES 6

1 FOR PASTRY: In a bowl, combine flour, sugar, salt, and orange zest. Using a pastry blender or 2 knives, cut in cold butter until mixture resembles coarse crumbs. Stir in 3–5 tablespoons (1½–2½ fl oz/ 45–75 ml) ice water, 1 tablespoon at a time, until dough coheres in a ball. Form into a disk. Wrap in plastic and refrigerate for 20 minutes.

2 Line lower oven rack with aluminum foil to catch any spills. Preheat oven to 425°F (220°C).

3 On a floured work surface, roll dough into a round about 12 inches (30 cm) in diameter and ⅛ inch (3 mm) thick. Transfer to a baking sheet.

4 FOR FILLING: In a large bowl, toss mulberries with sugar to taste, depending on tartness of berries. Stir in instant tapioca.

5 Pour berries into center of dough, leaving a rim of dough 2–3 inches (5–7.5 cm) wide. Fold excess dough over fruit, pleating as you go. Brush rim with some melted butter and sprinkle with sugar. Drizzle remaining butter over fruit. Bake until crust is browned, about 40 minutes.

Quince and Prune Tart

PASTRY

1 cup (5 oz/155 g) plus
2 tablespoons all-purpose
(plain) flour

pinch of salt

2 teaspoons sugar

1 tablespoon finely grated
orange zest

½ cup (4 oz/125 g) unsalted butter,
cut into small pieces

FILLING AND GLAZE

1 cup (6 oz/185 g) pitted prunes,
halved lengthwise

3 cups (24 fl oz/750 ml)
brewed Earl Grey tea

2 cups (16 fl oz/500 ml) Poached
Quinces in Wine Syrup, drained
and ½ cup (4 fl oz/125 ml) wine
syrup reserved (see page 33)

½ cup (4 fl oz/125 ml)
crème fraîche

1 egg

1 tablespoon sugar

whipped cream, for topping

SERVES 8

Yellow-skinned, tart, and crisp, quince tastes a bit like an apple and a bit like a pear. Prune is a tasty complement in this wintertime dessert.

1 FOR PASTRY: In a food processor, pulse flour, salt, sugar, and orange zest to blend. Add butter and pulse until mixture resembles fine crumbs. Add just enough water, about 2 tablespoons, to dampen crumbs. Remove from processor, bringing dough together in your hands. Form dough into a disk, wrap in plastic, and refrigerate for 30 minutes.

2 When cold, roll dough out ¼ inch (6 mm) thick and line a 9-inch (23-cm) tart pan with removable bottom. Trim excess and gently prick bottom and sides with a fork. Freeze until hardened, at least 20 minutes.

3 Preheat oven to 375°F (190°C). Line tart shell with parchment (baking) paper or aluminum foil and fill with pie weights or dried beans. Bake until sides are set, about 10 minutes. Remove weights and parchment or foil. Continue baking until bottom is set, 5 minutes longer. Remove from oven and let cool.

4 FOR FILLING AND GLAZE: In a saucepan, simmer prunes in tea until tender, 2–4 minutes. Drain and set aside. Arrange prunes and quinces in tart shell.

5 Whisk crème fraîche with egg and sugar. Pour over fruit and bake tart until custard is puffed and golden, about 35 minutes.

6 In a small saucepan, reduce reserved wine syrup over medium heat until a glaze consistency forms. When tart comes out of oven, brush top with syrup. Serve warm with whipped cream.

Pumpkin Pie

Pumpkin pie is a classic component of the traditional Thanksgiving menu. Whipped cream or vanilla ice cream are requisite toppings, although the pie is delicious all by itself.

PASTRY

1½ cups (7½ oz/235 g) all-purpose (plain) flour

¼ teaspoon salt

½ cup (4 oz/125 g) vegetable shortening

FILLING

2 cups (16 oz/500 g) pumpkin purée

3 eggs

1½ cups (12 fl oz/375 ml) heavy (double) cream

¾ cup (6 oz/185 g) firmly packed brown sugar

½ teaspoon salt

1½ teaspoons ground cinnamon

1 teaspoon ground ginger

½ teaspoon ground nutmeg

¼ teaspoon ground cloves

¼ teaspoon ground allspice

SERVES 8

1 FOR PASTRY: In a bowl, combine flour and salt. Using a pastry blender, 2 knives, or your fingertips, work shortening into flour until mixture resembles coarse crumbs. Sprinkle 3–4 tablespoons (1½–2 fl oz/ 45–60 ml) ice water over flour mixture, a tablespoon at a time, stirring lightly with a fork after each addition; use just enough water so that dough holds together. Shape dough into a thick disk. Wrap in plastic and refrigerate for 30 minutes.

2 Preheat oven to 450°F (230°C). On a lightly floured surface, roll out chilled dough ⅛ inch (3 mm) thick. Transfer to a 9-inch (23-cm) pie pan. Trim edges to fit and crimp edges, if desired. Prick pie shell several times with a fork. Line shell with aluminum foil and fill with pie weights or dried beans. Bake for 6 minutes. Remove weights and foil. Continue baking until pie shell just begins to brown, about 4 minutes longer.

3 FOR FILLING: In a large bowl, beat together pumpkin purée and eggs. Add cream, brown sugar, salt, and spices. Beat until smooth.

4 Pour filling into pie shell and bake for 10 minutes. Reduce oven temperature to 300°F (150°C) and continue baking until filling is nearly set, 30–40 minutes. (A sharp knife will come out almost clean, with traces of custard on it. Center of pie should not be completely firm.) Transfer to a wire rack and let cool.

Apple Tart with Chestnut Purée

The browned custard peeking out around the apples is the first hint that this is not an ordinary apple tart. It can take guests a surprisingly long time to guess that chestnuts are the secret ingredient.

PASTRY

½ cup (4 oz/125 g) plus 2 tablespoons unsalted butter, softened

¾ cup (3 oz/90 g) confectioners' (icing) sugar

pinch of salt

½ teaspoon cognac

1 egg, at room temperature, lightly beaten

1¾ cups (9 oz/280 g) unbleached all-purpose (plain) flour

FILLING AND GLAZE

3 apples

1 can (17½ oz/545 g) sweetened chestnut purée or *crème de marron*

2 eggs

⅓ cup (3½ oz/105 g) apricot preserves

SERVES 8

1 FOR PASTRY: In bowl of a stand mixer fitted with paddle attachment, beat butter. Add confectioners' sugar, salt, and cognac and mix well. With motor running, gradually add beaten egg. Beat until well blended, scraping down sides of bowl once or twice. Turn off mixer, add flour, and then mix on low speed until just combined. Dough will be soft and sticky. Wrap in plastic and flatten to a disk 1 inch (2.5 cm) thick. Refrigerate until firm, at least 1 hour.

2 Preheat to 375°F (190°C). Unwrap dough. If dough is very cold, beat with a rolling pin to make more malleable. On a lightly floured work surface, roll out dough into a 13-inch (33-cm) round about ⅛ inch (3 mm) thick. Carefully fit dough into a 9-inch (23-cm) fluted tart pan with removable bottom. Trim excess dough from around edges. Freeze tart shell for 20 minutes.

3 Line tart shell with parchment (baking) paper or aluminum foil and fill with pie weights or dried beans. Bake until sides are set, approximately 10 minutes.

Remove weights and parchment or foil. Continue baking until bottom is set, 5 minutes longer.

4 FOR FILLING AND GLAZE: Peel apples and cut in half vertically. Remove cores with a melon baller or sharp knife. Lay apple halves flat and cut into slices 1/16 inch (2 mm) thick, keeping slices together. Discard short end pieces.

5 In a bowl, whisk sweetened chestnut purée and eggs to combine. Pour mixture into tart shell. Arrange apple slices in overlapping, concentric circles to cover chestnut filling completely. Bake until chestnut purée is set and apples are browned, about 40 minutes.

6 Let cool in pan. Remove pan sides and base. In a small saucepan, combine apricot preserves with 2 tablespoons water. Warm over low heat until preserves melt, then strain through a fine-mesh sieve. Brush on top of tart.

breads & pastries

Bread making is more than a simple lesson in the chemistry of flour, salt, water, and yeast. Unlike other forms of baking, making bread and pastry is about the hands, not the head. It is a most pleasurable exercise—indeed the act of making a yeast loaf or quick bread can be as comforting as slicing and tasting the loaf itself.

Cardamom Fritters

The shape of these deep-fried Norwegian treats is said to resemble reindeer antlers. Serve them with mulled wine or with honey for dipping. In the summer months, they can be served with berries and cream.

3 eggs

¾ cup (5½ oz/170 g) superfine (caster) sugar

½ cup (4 fl oz/125 ml) heavy (double) cream, whipped to soft peaks

½ cup (4 oz/125 g) unsalted butter, melted and slightly cooled

2 tablespoons Aquavit or brandy

1 teaspoon finely grated lemon zest

½ teaspoon crushed cardamom seeds

4½ cups (18 oz/560 g) self-rising flour

peanut oil or vegetable oil, for frying

MAKES ABOUT 5 DOZEN

1 In a large bowl, use an electric mixer at medium-high speed to whisk eggs and sugar until fluffy and light, 7–9 minutes. Add whipped cream, melted butter, Aquavit, lemon zest, and cardamom, folding until blended. Sift flour and gradually fold into mixture in 3 or 4 additions until blended. Turn out dough onto a floured work surface and, with floured hands, knead several times until smooth. Divide dough into 2 equal portions. Form each portion into a flattened disk, wrap in plastic, and refrigerate until firm, at least overnight or up to 2 days.

2 Working with 1 portion at a time, roll out chilled dough on a lightly floured surface to a thickness of about ⅜ inch (1 cm). Cut dough into strips 4 inches (10 cm) long. Using kitchen shears or a sharp knife, nick each strip 4 or 5 times along one side. Form each strip into a ring with nicked edge facing out and press ends together to seal. Repeat with remaining dough, then gather up scraps, reroll, and cut out additional strips.

3 In a deep fryer or heavy saucepan, pour at least 2 inches (5 cm) oil. Heat to 375°F (190°C) on a deep-frying thermometer.

4 Working in batches, fry the rings 2 or 3 at a time, turning once, until crisp and golden brown, 1–2 minutes total. Drain well on paper towels. Repeat with remaining rings. Serve warm or at room temperature. Store in an airtight container lined with paper towels.

Easter Bread with Almond Icing

½ cup (4 fl oz/125 ml) whole milk

2½ teaspoons (1 envelope) active dry yeast

2⅔ cups (13½ oz/420 g) unbleached all-purpose (plain) flour

2 whole eggs, plus 1 egg yolk

⅓ cup (3 oz/90 g) granulated sugar

½ cup (4 oz/125 g) unsalted butter, melted

½ teaspoon salt

1 teaspoon *each* vanilla extract (essence) and grated lemon zest

½ cup (3 oz/90 g) *each* dark raisins and golden raisins (sultanas)

ALMOND ICING
½ cup (2½ oz/75 g) whole blanched almonds

½ cup (4 oz/125 g) granulated sugar

1 tablespoon cornstarch (cornflour)

2 egg whites

½ cup (2 oz/60 g) sliced almonds

confectioners' (icing) sugar, for dusting

SERVES 12

In Italy, a traditional Italian Easter bread similar to panettone is baked in the shape of a *colomba pasquale* or Easter dove, a symbol of the Resurrection. Because the dove-shaped molds are difficult to find outside Italy, here the colomba is formed in a loaf pan. The almond icing is typical of mass-produced colombas, but it adds a perfect crunch.

1 In a small saucepan over low heat, warm milk to lukewarm, about 100°F (38°C). Transfer milk to a small bowl. Sprinkle yeast on surface of milk and let stand for 2 minutes, then stir yeast into milk to dissolve. Stir in ⅔ cup (3½ oz/ 105 g) flour. Cover with plastic wrap and let sit in a warm place until doubled, 30 minutes.

2 In bowl of a stand mixer, whisk eggs and egg yolk together. Whisk in granulated sugar, then melted butter. Using a rubber spatula, stir in salt, vanilla, lemon zest, and yeast mixture. Gradually stir in remaining 2 cups (10 oz/315 g) flour.

3 Using a dough hook, beat on low speed until dough is smooth and elastic, about 5 minutes. Beat in raisins.

4 Scrape dough into a large buttered bowl. Cover with buttered plastic wrap and let rise in a warm place until doubled in bulk, about 1 hour.

5 Grease two 8½-by-4½-inch (21.5-by-11.5-cm) loaf pans. Turn dough out onto a lightly floured surface and pat flat. Cut in half. Roll each half into a 10-by-7-inch (25-by-18-cm) rec- tangle. Roll up like jelly rolls and place seam side down in loaf pans. Cover loosely with buttered plastic wrap and let rise in a warm place until doubled in bulk, about 45 minutes.

6 Preheat oven to 375°F (190°C).

7 FOR ALMOND ICING: In a food proces- sor, combine almonds, granulated sugar, cornstarch, and egg whites. Process to a smooth paste. Carefully spread icing on risen loaves to avoid deflating them. Sprinkle with sliced almonds and confec- tioners' sugar.

8 Bake until well risen and baked through, about 30 minutes. Let cool in pans on a wire rack. Unmold. If almonds fall off, replace. Dust with additional confectioners' sugar.

Hot Cross Buns

½ cup (4 oz/125 ml) warm milk

1 package active dry yeast

½ teaspoon plus ¼ cup (2 oz/60 g) granulated sugar

2 cups (10 oz/315 g) all-purpose (plain) flour, plus more if needed

½ teaspoon ground allspice

¼ teaspoon ground cinnamon

½ teaspoon salt

5 tablespoons (2½ oz/75 g) unsalted butter, cut into small pieces and softened

1 egg

2 tablespoons golden raisins (sultanas)

2 tablespoons *each* diced candied citron and diced candied orange peel

GLAZE AND PASTE

1 egg

4 tablespoons (2 oz/60 g) superfine (caster) sugar

3 tablespoons all-purpose (plain) flour

MAKES 12

These sweet rolls are an Eastertime tradition, although they are easy to bake and eat any time of year.

1 In bowl of a stand mixer, stir together milk, yeast, and ½ teaspoon granulated sugar. Set aside until foamy, about 5 minutes.

2 In another bowl, mix together 2 cups flour, allspice, cinnamon, salt, and remaining ¼ cup granulated sugar. Add half of flour mixture to mixer and combine using paddle attachment. Mix in butter and egg. Add remaining flour mixture and combine until a soft dough forms.

3 Change to a dough hook and knead until dough is smooth and elastic, about 10 minutes. Add more flour if needed, 1 tablespoon at a time (up to ¼ cup/ 1½ oz/45 g), to keep dough from being sticky. Transfer to a lightly oiled large bowl; turn to coat. Cover with plastic wrap; let rise in a warm, draft-free place until doubled in bulk, about 1½ hours.

4 Punch down dough and knead in raisins and candied fruits. Shape dough into a 12-inch (30-cm) log and cut into 12 equal pieces. Cover with plastic wrap and let rest for 10 minutes. Shape each piece into a ball and arrange 1½ inches (4 cm) apart on a baking sheet lined with parchment (baking) paper. Cover buns and let rise in a warm place until doubled in bulk, about 45 minutes.

5 Preheat oven to 400°F (200°C).

6 FOR GLAZE AND PASTE: In a small bowl, mix together egg and 3 tablespoons superfine sugar to make glaze. In another bowl, combine 3 tablespoons flour, 1 tablespoon superfine sugar, and 3 tablespoons water to make a smooth paste. Fill a pastry bag fitted with a small tip with paste. Brush buns with egg glaze. Pipe a cross onto each. Bake until golden, 10–12 minutes. Serve warm.

Toasted Banana Bread

2 cups (8 oz/250 g) sifted
all-purpose (plain) flour

1 teaspoon baking powder

½ teaspoon salt

6 tablespoons (3 oz/90 g)
unsalted butter

½ cup (4 oz/125 g) sugar

2 eggs, lightly beaten

1 cup (8 oz/250 g) mashed ripe
bananas (about 2 bananas)

MAKES 1 LOAF, ABOUT 10 SLICES

This old-fashioned loaf is not too sweet. Toasting the slices provides a delicious contrast between the crunchy exterior and soft interior. Serve with butter and honey or with cream cheese. This bread can be made a day ahead, especially if toasting.

1 Preheat oven to 350°F (180°C). Grease a 9-by-5-by-3-inch (23-by-13-by-7.5-cm) loaf pan.

2 In a bowl, use a whisk to combine flour, baking powder, and salt. Cream butter and sugar until light and fluffy, either by hand or in a stand mixer on medium speed. Gradually add eggs, mixing to combine. Stir in mashed bananas and flour mixture by thirds. Pour batter into prepared loaf pan.

3 Bake until loaf starts to pull away from edges of pan, about 50 minutes. Let bread stand in pan for 5–10 minutes, then turn it out onto a wire rack to cool completely.

4 Slice and toast on a hot griddle or in a toaster oven.

Chocolate Brioches

Perfect on their own, brioches also serve well as the base for elegant desserts. Slice them and top with ice cream and chocolate shavings, or butter the slices and toast them, then layer with raspberries and whipped cream.

1 package (¼ oz/7 g) active dry yeast

3 tablespoons lukewarm milk (100°–110°F/38°–43°C)

4 cups (1¼ lb/625 g) all-purpose (plain) flour, plus more if needed

⅓ cup (1 oz/30 g) cocoa powder

½ cup (4 oz/125 g) sugar

1 teaspoon salt

7 eggs, at room temperature, lightly beaten

1 cup (8 oz/250 g) unsalted butter, softened

4 oz (125 g) bittersweet chocolate, chopped in ¼-inch (6-mm) pieces

vegetable oil for coating

1 egg beaten with 1 tablespoon water, for egg wash

MAKES FOURTEEN 2½-INCH (6-CM) BRIOCHES

1 In a liquid measuring pitcher, combine yeast and milk. Stir until dissolved. Let stand until foamy, 5–10 minutes.

2 In bowl of a standing mixer fitted with dough hook, combine flour, cocoa powder, sugar, and salt. Add yeast mixture and eggs. Beat on medium-low speed until ingredients are blended and dough is smooth, about 5 minutes. With machine running, add butter, 1–2 tablespoons at a time, blending well after each addition. Continue mixing until dough is shiny and elastic and begins to pull away from sides of bowl, 4–5 minutes. If dough does not pull away from sides, mix in additional flour 2 tablespoons at a time. Do not add too much; dough should be sticky. Mix in chopped chocolate.

3 Coat a large bowl lightly with vegetable oil. Transfer dough to bowl and cover with plastic wrap. Let rise until nearly doubled in volume, about 2 hours. Transfer dough to a lightly floured surface. Punch down and shape into a ball. Return dough to oiled bowl, cover with plastic wrap, and let rise in refrigerator overnight.

4 Remove dough from refrigerator, punch down, and transfer to a lightly floured work surface. Divide dough in half, then divide each half into 7 equal-sized pieces. Roll each piece into a ball and place smooth side up in paper brioche or panettone molds. Place filled molds on a baking sheet and cover loosely with plastic wrap. Let rise again at room temperature until almost doubled in size, 1½–2 hours.

5 Meanwhile, preheat oven to 350°F (180°C). Lightly brush dough with egg wash. Bake until brioches have a hollow sound when tapped, about 35 minutes. Transfer to a wire rack and let cool.

index

acknowledgements

Weldon Owen would like to thank the former TASTE magazine editorial and design teams for their creative efforts. Special thanks to the many talented authors and photographers who contributed so greatly to this book. And, finally, thanks to Richard Van Oosterhout, Juli Vendzules, Stephanie Owen, Tanya Henry, Joan Olson, Maggie Ruggiero, and Kate Krader for their valuable assistance.

credits

AUTHORS: ALISON ATTENBOROUGH: Page 38; GEORGEANNE BRENNAN: Pages 15, 19, 20, 37; CHAMPAGNE VEUVE CLICQUOT: Page 58; CHEF JOEL CHAPOULIER: Page 99; MARION CUNNINGHAM: Page 109; SARA DESERAN: Pages 41, 69, 73; FRAN GAGE: Pages 16, 66, 94, 100, 110; JOYCE GOLDSTEIN: Page 47; ANDY HARRIS: Page 28; ELIZABETH LUARD: Pages 57, 86, 89, 90, 115; EMILY LUCHETTI: Pages 74, 77; DEBORAH MADISON: Pages 33, 34, 51, 81, 103, 106; DONATA MAGGIPINTO: Page 23; GEORGE MAHAFFEY: Page 44; NICK MALGIERI: Pages 65, 116; CHEF GILLES MARCHAL: Page 54; JAMIE OLIVER: Page 24; MAGGIE RUGGIERO: Page 121; VICTORIA SPENCER: Pages 93, 122; MARIMAR TORRES: Pages 61, 82; ROBYN VALARIK: Pages 48, 78, 85, 125; CHUCK WILLIAMS: Page 27.

PHOTOGRAPHERS: ANTONIS ACHILLEOS: Pages 50, 52, 53, 80; BURCU AVSAR: Pages 112, 120; QUENTIN BACON: Page 40; LEIGH BEISCH: Pages 1, 45, 46, 118 (top left); BEATRIZ DA COSTA: Pages 17, 64, 67, 101, 117; MICHAEL FREEMAN: Page 31 (top left, top right, bottom left, bottom right); DANA GALLAGHER: Endpapers, Page 6; JOHN KERNICK: Pages 92, 123; DAVID LOFTUS: Pages 9 (top right), 10, 11, 25, 29, 30, 39, 68, 70, 71, 72, 95, 102, 111, 118 (bottom left, bottom right); WILLIAM MEPPEM: Pages 2, 8, 9 (top left, bottom left, bottom right), 26, 32, 35, 42, 55, 59, 60, 83, 98, 104, 105, 107, 118 (top right); MINH + WASS: Pages 49, 62, 79, 84, 96, 108, 124; AMY NEUNSINGER: Pages 12, 22; VICTORIA PEARSON: Pages 14, 18, 21, 36, 119; ANNA WILLIAMS: Pages 56, 75, 76, 87, 88, 91, 114.

WILLIAMS-SONOMA INC.
Founder & Vice Chairman: Chuck Williams

WILLIAMS-SONOMA TASTE
Editor-in-Chief: Andy Harris
Art Director: Emma Ross
Original Design: Martin Welch

WELDON OWEN INC.
Chief Executive Officer: John Owen
President: Terry Newell
Chief Operating Officer: Larry Partington
Vice President International Sales: Stuart Laurence
Sales Manager: Emily Jahn
Creative Director: Gaye Allen
Publisher: Hannah Rahill
Associate Creative Director: Leslie Harrington
Associate Publisher: Val Cipollone
Art Director: Kari Ontko, India Ink
Consulting Editor: Victoria Spencer
Assistant Editor: Mitch Goldman
Copy Editor and Proofreader: Desne Ahlers
Indexer: Ken DellaPenta
Production: Chris Hemesath, Teri Bell

CAKES, COOKIES, PIES & TARTS
Conceived and produced by Weldon Owen Inc.
814 Montgomery Street, San Francisco, CA 94133
In collaboration with Williams-Sonoma Inc.
3250 Van Ness Avenue, San Francisco, CA 94109

Printed in China by Midas Printing Limited

A WELDON OWEN PRODUCTION

First printed in 2003
10 9 8 7 6 5 4 3 2 1

Library of Congress Cataloging-in-Publication Data is available

ISBN 1-740895-15-0